You, God, and your Dog

Your relationship with God is a lot like your
dog's relationship with you.

Joseph Brincku

You, God, and Your Dog

Joseph Brincku

You, God, and Your Dog

Table of Contents

You, God, and Your Dog

Chapter 1: You, God, and your Dog

As my wife and I drove to the dog breeder, we had relatively low expectations for finding just the right pet to add to our family. We arrived at the breeder and met the mom dog and dad dog, who had just given birth to a litter of 5 puppies. We liked the parents, so we began to get excited about maybe finding the right one. All of the puppies were spoken for except for the smallest, the runt of the litter, if you will. We were told that if we wanted a puppy that day, it would have to be him or nothing at all. With no real expectations, we went and took a look at all 5 of the pre-weened little wonders. Four of them crawled over each other and begged for our attention. One sat silently in the corner of the playpen where they were kept. One glance and I knew; That was our runt.

So even though we knew he was the most unwanted of pups, we decided to take a chance and keep him as ours. We searched for him, wanted him, and we claimed him.

The drive home that first trip was nothing short of amazing. He sat quietly in my wife's arms with her fingers in his mouth to keep him calm. That evening, I slept on the couch while he slept on the floor, all while I had my hand over him to keep him comfy and secure. Within a few months, He grew to be 120 pounds and filled our lives with joy. But wait . . . we provided for him, we gave him security, we provide him with food and a place to live, we provided him with everything, YET it was us who were given the joy.

The cute little furry puppy that I picked out of a litter of five has turned out to be one of my best buds. My black Labrador that we named Max consistently gives me more than I could imagine any 'human' can offer. I know that I speak from experience that my little buddy Max . . . hungers to be with me . . . waits for me to be with him . . . He chooses to show obedience to me. He strives to overachieve above my expectations. You can just see it in his eyes when he stares at you. I am his Master, and it is me who receives the joy from his existence.

At the start of writing this book, Max turns eleven, and as he struggles to get up and has trouble breathing, we notice that he is aging quickly. It won't be too much longer that he will come to the end of his life and will leave us. He will be abundantly missed and will leave a hole in my heart when that time comes. His life with us has caused me to ponder a profound yet straightforward thought about life and eternity. What would Heaven look like for Max? And then, it caused me to see some of the similarities of our life with our pets and how God treats us. It has revealed some amazing things to me that may bring it home: why are we here? (Us Humans that is) Has Max inadvertently taught me the meaning of life?

Could it be that we may view Heaven incorrectly? Could it be that we may view God incorrectly? What if we took a look at God through a dog's eyes? A look at how our relationship with God is much like our relationship with our beloved pets. Join me in the exploration of You, God, and your Dog.

Chapter 2: Choosing a Puppy

For us, the search for Max started with the loss of another Family Dog that we had. Ben was his name. He was a Labrador, just like Max. One day, Ben stopped eating. We waited two days because it was relatively normal for him not to eat for a day or two. But after day two, we began to get worried and took him to the Veterinarian. They gave him intravenous fluids and sent us home. We found him on the floor with little to no strength the following day. We rushed him to the hospital, and they thought that he might have a turned stomach. They did some x-ray testing and told us that he had to undergo immediate surgery. We approved of the operation, and away he went. After the procedure was over, they told us the news that they were wrong and that he did not have a turned stomach. He needed to stay the night at the hospital to recover as he was so weak. In the morning, we got the news that Ben had died overnight. He was only four years old. We were heartbroken and started to search for a new family member immediately. It had to be just the right one to replace our beloved Ben.

So, you want a new puppy? Then you must search for one that is just right. You must search for one that you want. If you find the right one, you will be rewarded with many years of loyalty.

Many of us believe that WE find God. I mean, who do we think that we are? Finding God? Do we believe that God is lost enough so that we need to seek him out and find him? The fact is that God is always searching and seeking us. He desires to be with us. In Luke 19, Jesus says, "the Son of man came to seek and save the lost." We give a pat on our backs when we say that we 'found God', but the reality is that God seeks us and finds us. He chooses us.

So just like a new pet owner goes on the search for a new addition to the Family, God searches for us. God picks us out, and when he snatches us up into his arms, we are just like a little puppy with no idea of who has given shelter. All we know is that we feel safe, and much like the little puppy that we choose for a pet, God watches over us as we learn what it is to be one of those in his kingdom.

For the first few days with God, we start to see how powerful he is. We follow him everywhere he goes. We want to be with him all of the time; we want to walk with him wherever we go. We stare at him and enjoy his presence.

In these first moments of being with God, we begin to formulate loyalty. Although we do not have a full grasp of how and why we know that we want to be loyal and it makes us feel so good that we wag our tail . . . Well, you get the point. (pointer) – I couldn't help myself.

Isn't it good to know that God seeks us out? I know that when I learned this, it gave me a big smile. How is it that the God who created the Universe was actively searching for communion with me? And then I was left with . . . Why? So while I felt relatively small in that I had no place to search for God, it quickly became so much more important for God to search for little ole me. I AM that important to him, and in knowing this, I am unique, But not special for my purpose but his. WOW, that is enlightening.

Being chosen by God gives me the worth that I could never get by any means on my own. And just like the new little puppy that you choose to be your companion, we quickly learn that God wanting us and wanting to be with us is more important than anything. We will eventually learn to live for it, and oddly enough, we will enjoy loving with eyes wide shut. No matter what happens, we will love our Master, the one who snatched us up and keeps us safe in his arms.

So what about "free will"? If God chooses us and we don't choose him, where is our free will? I believe that both are possible. That God chooses us for Salvation, and we also choose God. When you choose your little puppy, it chooses to love you. Whether you believe it or not, your new puppy decides not to like you as much as it can choose to like you. Of course, he is predestined to love the one that becomes his Master, and so the choice is clear and easy, but it is a choice. So although we choose him because he is destined to love us, he also makes a choice. The hole in his life is filled with his Master and being a dutiful servant to his Master for the rest of his life.

Spoken only hours before his Death Jesus spoke these words.

John 15:16 "You did not choose me, but I chose you and appointed you so that you might go and bear fruit, Fruit that will last, and so that whatever you ask in my name the Father will give you."

The basic premise of this verse is that Jesus chose his Apostles and that they are to bear fruit. But did he really choose them? Andrew followed Jesus immediately, and then he went to Peter and brought him to Jesus. Most of the Apostles were not given a choice to follow; they just did. It does not seem like Jesus chose them but rather the other way around. Jesus chose the Apostles, and they chose Jesus by following him. See, both can be true. And just like your new little puppy, they were chosen because they were the right people, and they were predestined to be the followers, so the choice to follow was an easy one for them.

I believe that the words of Jesus were to give us an easier time in carrying his cross. If we are the chooser than when we fall, it is all on us. But if we are the chosen, when we fall, the chooser is at fault. Bearing fruit means that we are to take up the cross when Jesus died, and he knew how hard that would be. And so, he followed it up by saying that what we want will be given to us. So, pick up the cross and help Jesus carry it for as long as you can, and if you have to pause to catch your breath, Jesus understands. Ask when you need help, and he will be there for you. This is so comforting!

You, God, and Your Dog

Chapter 3:
Stages of Life, Stages of Learning, Stages of Christianity

When Max joined our home as a puppy, he was a delight. On our way home from the breeder, I remember that he sat in my wife's arms, and she put her fingers in his mouth and he was immediately content with it. He was so small that this was about the extent of what he could do. When we got home with him the first day, I also remember that we took him to his new backyard and let him investigate. I took a picture of him while he walked in the grass, and the grass was taller than he was. Such a tiny puppy, yet so quickly, they change into young dogs and then, mature animals.

What do you expect from your new puppy? Do you expect your new puppy of 8-10 weeks of age to be able to hold taking a bathroom break until he is outside? Probably not. Do you expect that your new puppy will go and fetch his toy for you to play with him? Probably not. Do you expect your new puppy to behave while you are outside of the house? Probably not. The fact is that when a puppy is just brought into your home for the first time, we expect very little of it. It is good enough for him to spend time with us, play around a little, and cuddle. God treats us this way as well.

When we are a new Christian, God will not

expect us to solve World problems. God isn't going to ask you to step too far outside of your comfort zone. He will treat you like you treat your little puppy. He just wants you and him to get to know each other and for you to trust him. He wants you to know that he has your best interest at heart, and he will provide for you.

As your puppy grows, he enters years one through three. These are challenging times for those of us who have owned a dog. These are the times when you leave the room for what seems to be seconds and come back, and the garbage is all over the kitchen. And don't even get me started on leaving a 2-year-old dog in your home outside of his cage while you go to the store. You will most likely come back to your new couch in 1,297 pieces! It is during these years that your dog learns. And if you did not take the time to reprimand and teach him during these years, the next 5-10 years will be awful for you as a pet owner because you will be living with a wild animal instead of a Family pet.

After a period of being a "baby Christian", we have time to learn. This is our time to read the Bible and get acquainted with who God is and what we are tasked to do here on Earth.

2 Timothy 3:16-17 says "All Scripture is breathed out by God and profitable for teaching, for reproof, for correction, and for training in righteousness, that the man of God may be competent, equipped for every good work."

And then in

Mathew 4:4 Jesus says, "Man shall not live by bread alone, but by every word that comes from the mouth of God."

So, we take time to read the Word, and we learn. But left to our own devices, we turn into that puppy that eats everything that he is not supposed to touch, let alone chew up. This is when God gently reminds us of what we have done wrong. The Holy Spirit, which now starts to guide our life nudges us in the direction that God wants us to move. We begin to have the ability to see wrong in our lives, and we are compelled to correct them. This usually is when we desire to remove the unclean from our lives, and we begin to seek goodness. It is important to note that we cannot start to feel the Holy until we begin to read the

Word. God cannot speak to you unless you are in communion with Him, and he cannot be in communion with you until you read his Word. Being that 2 Timothy says that all scripture is breathed out of God, it stands that the Bible is, therefore, God's way to communicate with you. And just like your 1-3-year-old pet, you too will be reprimanded.

Revelation 3:19 says "Those whom I love, I reprove and discipline, so be zealous and repent."

God needs us to be trainable during this time of learning. He needs us to accept his nudges, and he needs us to be willing to change. For example, your pet desires to chew up your baseboards in the house; trust me, he does. This makes him happy! He feels that this is why he was born. It is up to you to teach him that this is unacceptable, and in turn, when he stops, he can grow into a new and more trustworthy part of the household. God does the same for us, and once you start to identify portions of your life as sin, you will be relieved to make changes, and it will feel so good.

As your dog ages, this is when most pet owners see a true benefit of being a dog owner. This is when your dog looks to you for direction and moves on command. This is when your dog is ready to do whatever it is that you speak. It is much less about what he wants to do, which is probably sleeping in a corner, eating from time to time, and chewing on your socks. At this 'after three' age, your dog becomes more than just a pet but has transitioned into a true part of the family.

So too, it is like our relationship with God. It might not take three years, so the time frames are irrelevant, but there is most certainly a beginning of Christianity, learning to live for Christ phase of Christianity, and a mature Christian phase. All of that discipline pays off for you as a dog owner, and I submit that the same is true for God with us. He delights in us transitioning out of a person he chose, to a chosen person.

Hebrews 12:11 says "For the moment all discipline seems painful rather than pleasant, but later it yields the peaceful fruit of righteousness to those who have been trained by it."

This is when as mature Christians we are ready to do the work of God. This is when we can hear the word of God telling us to act, telling us what he desires us to do. The Holy Spirit places this upon your heart, and it is not until you are a mature

Christian that you can act on it and succeed in doing it. It is essential to wait for God to turn us from a lump of coal into a diamond as if we do; we are so much more powerful when we act. This is when God looks down on us and sees a good and faithful servant. And this is also when God expands what he asks us to achieve.

So, if you are the type of person who wants to be full in with God and his plan, take the time to be a baby first, one who can be taught, and then you will see progress.

Mark 16:15 "Jesus said Go into the entire world and proclaim the gospel to the whole creation."

Chapter 4: Learning to Sit

It wasn't very long after we brought him home that our Max learned his name. Max this, Max that. He would lift his ears whenever he heard his name and wait for what it was that we said next. I remember just saying "Max . . ." with a long pause and he would stare at me with such intent. Nothing else around him was important; he would stare and stare.

God knows our name personally; he gave it to us before we were created. The Lamb's Book of Life is a record containing the names of those who have overcome sin through accepting Jesus as Lord. In other words, the Book of Life is the list of the redeemed—those who will live with God forever in Heaven. So, not only does God seek you out, but he knows you, and he calls you by your name. He enters it into his book of those who will be with him in Paradise! In Revelation chapter 3, it is written, "and your name is written in the book of life, and that God will acknowledge you as one of his own". Is it not the most amazing thing that God calls us by name? How important must I be that the God who created all things knows me by name and writes that name in his book?

Along with his name, one of the first things that Max learned was how to sit. We spent about an hour with him the first time we tried to teach him how to sit, and within a few sessions of doing this, he had easily mastered the ability to sit when we asked him to sit. So why is sitting one of the first things we teach our dogs?

Psalms 46:10 "Be still and know that I am God"

God spoke this to Israel amidst a war that they were in. He did not ask them to fight to the death; he asked them to be still. What a lesson this is in such a small verse in the Bible. The message isn't really about staying still, the message is, "Know that I am God, and sometimes I want you to believe that and just be still; I got this."

I submit that one of the first things that you learn when you start your walk with God is to 'sit'. When you sit down and wait to hear the following words from your Master, you have the opportunity to truly listen.

I heard a while back that it is always best to "Shut Up and Wait for God to Speak". And it is so true. Until we sit and listen, we cannot hear what God wants us to hear, and we cannot truly show that we know that he is God. If we always speak, how can God get a word in edgewise, and sometimes it is best just to let God fight for us. In the fast-paced society we live in, our lives are filled with so much nonsense. Whether it is social media or the TV or some other pointless waste of time, we are inundated with ways to waste our existence! God wants us to be fierce.

2 Timothy 4:17 "But the Lord stood at my side and gave me strength so that through me the message might be fully proclaimed and all the Gentiles might hear it. And I was delivered from the lion's mouth."

Paul says this while he had a trial which ultimately could lead to him being fed to the lions as Daniel was. He had no support from Friends or relatives; he was alone. However, Paul wrote this as he knew that God was with him, and he was not alone. Paul was weak within himself, and in this trying time, he took comfort and strength knowing that the Lord was with him. All so that he could proclaim the message. And what proof do we have that God was with him and that Paul was given strength and that he did spread the word? Read your Bible; the evidence is in the words on the page. Two thousand years later we read the powerful message given to us by Paul, who God strengthened.

And so, you too, should never feel alone. Jesus wants us to be relevant, and He wants us to be successful, maybe not monetarily successful, but successful in showing others his love through our actions. When you sit, you can tune out all of the everyday clouds and start to do what God intends you to do. Who knew that just sitting could be so invigorating and liberating?

Have you ever noticed that your dog will seek you out and lay next to you? He loves your company. What your dog is doing by lying next to you is saying that he feels close to you and shows you affection. But most of all, he is saying, I go where you lead, and if laying down next to you is where I am to be at this very moment, then I am ok with that.

In Proverbs 6:16-19, God says that he hates "pride". God does not want you to do what you want to do; he wants you to die to yourself and do what he wants you to do. God delights in you following his direction, sitting/laying, and listening, and he loves you so much that he gives you the free will to follow or go astray. It is amazing! But going back to 2 Timothy 4:17, there will be time to take action. God will direct you to no longer sit or lay down; he will ask you to act on something. He knows that the time is right for you, so do what you hear him say. He will guide you and help you; it is promised to us! Godspeed!

Chapter 5: Learning to Speak – And Learning when to be Quiet

Max was one of the quietest dogs that we have ever experienced. Being a Labrador, it was not unexpected for him to sit and be quiet for hours. For Max, I believe that it boiled down to his love for us and how instead of whining or barking, he would rather have your fingers in his mouth. On his first night with us, we had no dog crate for him, and we did not want him to roam around during the night and possibly get into something that would hurt him. Yes, we were like brand new parents worrying about our new little boy. Our couch had two ottomans to rest your feet on, so I brought them together to form a makeshift bed. I decided to sleep on the ottomans that first evening, and I laid Max at my side on the floor. I put my arm to the side, and as long as he had my fingers in his mouth, he stayed right there and slept the whole night through. From day one, he was a joy!

All dogs will eventually make their first little yapping noise. Oh, how cute! Those little puppy growls can be the most adorable sounds ever. But then your little puppy becomes a dog, and when he barks, it sounds like the walls will cave in. As a homeowner with a Family, I love when my dog barks at the door when someone knocks. It tells the people outside that a ferocious dog protects my home, which is a good thing. However, if you live in an apartment and your dog barks 24 hours a day, that is less desirable.

Sometimes we want our little puppy to make those cute noises, and sometimes we want our grown-up dog to bark and other times, most of the times; we want them to be quiet.

Psalm 150:1-6 "Praise God in his sanctuary; praise him in his mighty heavens. Praise him for his acts of power; praise him for his surpassing greatness. Praise him with the clash of cymbals, praise him with resounding cymbals. Let everything that has breath praise the LORD."

God LOVES to hear us praise his name! He loves to hear our worship. I submit that the main reason for us to be on the Earth is to learn how to praise the name of our Lord. We have 60, 70, 80, even 90 or 100 years to learn how to praise God the way that he calls us to. When we praise his name, his heart is filled with joy and in turn, our hearts are filled with his spirit of joy. If anyone has worshipped at a spirit-filled Church, they will know what I am about to say. The moment you let go of yourself and genuinely worship with song, hands held high, eyes weeping, and voices singing high is the most centralized connection to Heaven that we can feel here on Earth. That moment when we do the above is what most consider the freest that they will ever feel. That joy is wonderful, but it is also fleeting. Once we stop the praise, we often return to the harsh World, and our true feeling of joy evaporates into the wind.

So, God wants us to speak. He wants us to speak his name. He wants us to praise his worthiness. BUT he also wants us to be silent at times. There are genuinely times when you must be quiet. Give this thought. How much time do you spend speaking to God during your prayer time? Asking God? And sometimes pleading with God? Try this next time you pray. - Speak nothing. Just concentrate on the holiness of God. Submit your voice to your ears and mind. Concentrate, and I just know that you will hear from your Lord. So many people tell me that they never "hear from God" and that God "does not speak to them," and it is my inner thought to ask them if they take time to be quiet and listen for his command.

If you are like that dog that barks all of the time when you are around others, you will quite frankly be just an annoyance. Barking dogs will often scare other people, quiet dogs who wait to be pet are often the ones that are approached by others. Give that thought. I know that I often find myself barking at others, and this is a mistake that I often make and am trying to rectify.

Sometimes God can use you more easily if you are just quiet and let others speak. For example, if you wait for someone to ask you what is that light inside of you, you can tell them, and they will have open ears to hear. But if you are consistently barking at people about things, they will often be afraid of you and will tune you out.

So, when God needs you to be a protector, he will ask you to bark. And he loves to hear you bark praise. And sometimes, he just wants you to be quiet so that he can teach you and then use you. That is the good news; God has a purpose for your life!

Psalm 57:2 says, "I cry out to God Most High, to God who fulfills his purpose for me."

What does this mean? Firstly, David says that God is sufficient for all of our needs as he is the "most high" and that no one is above him. And secondly, David is saying that God is able. God is not only able to supply for me, but he provides purpose for me, and then he nudges me to accomplish all that is purposed for me in my life.

So today, take comfort in knowing that God loves your praise; it is sweet music to his ears! And take comfort in knowing that the purpose that God has led you to will be fulfilled not because of what you will need to do to accomplish it but because he has ordained it as so. God is able; you are his vessel. So let him lead you where you are to go but know that you will need to die to yourself and take up his cross where he left it for you.

How do you know that you are not finding the purpose that God has for you? Be prepared for truth here . . . If you live in unrepentant sin, you are not living a Godly purpose-filled life. I know that this is hard, and the modern Church teaches that we are all sinners and only by Jesus are we to gain salvation, but I submit that our lives are equally as important.

Search your life and lifestyle and identify the area/s which you can point to that are sinful. If you find some, you are living without purpose. If you feel like you are standing still in life, then you are probably not living a Godly purpose-driven life. If you desperately feel like you need to make a change, this is an important sign that you are not living in God's purpose for your life. If you are not excited about your direction, take a moment to give it thought, as this is probably another clue that you are not on God's path for your life.

So how is it that we are to find God's purpose?
Pray
Pray
Pray
and
Read
Read
Read
(the Bible).

Psalm 119:105 says, "Your word is a lamp to my feet and a light to my path."

God speaks to us through the Bible, so it is so important to read his word to understand and be able to hear what he is trying to say to you.

Another way to hear God's purpose is to get alone for a while and clear your mind. He often finds a quiet moment to whisper things to you and if you are in a quiet place, you can hear what he has to say. But, most importantly, you need to trust God!

Psalm 23:2-3 says, "He leads me beside still waters. He restores my

soul. He leads me in paths of righteousness for his name's sake."

So, if you simply trust God, it will set you free. He will give you something that you are passionate about, and if you follow his path and not your own, you will feel peace and know that you are living to God's purpose for your life.

Chapter 6: It's Ok not knowing much

Max was very smart and could understand a lot of what we said. His way of communicating with us was to stare at the wall; this meant; "I need something." Whether that was that he was hungry or needed to go outside or wanted to play, he would stare at the wall while standing right next to you until you asked a question, and if you said the right thing, he would kind of sneeze. Somehow my wife would always be in tune with him enough to know what he wanted; it took me a few tries to guess what he was trying to tell me. Max knew a lot of commands, but he also knew quite a few sentences as well. "Do you want to go for a ride?" was his favorite. It got so all that I had to do was to say, "Do you?" and his ears would perk up and wait for the rest of the statement.

The average dog knows around 100 words. If you have a very smart dog, they can learn up to 165 words. The average person knows approximately 30,000 words. WOW, you know 30,000 words, and that lovable little fur buddy of yours only knows 100 words, YET you love that little guy with all of your might!

Psalms 139:4 "Before a word is on my tongue you, Lord, know it completely."

Have you ever given thought to the number of words that God knows? I submit that God knows every word ever spoken and every thought ever thought of. He is omnipotent and all-knowing. The English Dictionary has roughly 172,000 words in current use and 48,000 words that have been deleted. That totals over 220,000 English Words! God knows every word in the Dictionary. There are 6500 spoken languages in the History of the World, and it would be safe to assume that each of them has about as many words as the English Dictionary, so this makes the combined total of all words at around 1.5 billion words in all of the World. God knows them all.

NOW, let's blow some minds. If God knows all Words and he is all-knowing, he then would not only know all words but would also know all of the words ever spoken. He would have heard all of the words ever spoken in all of history. The average person speaks 370 million words in his lifetime, and approximately 107 billion people have lived on this earth, this means that there are a total of 39,590,000,000,000,000,000 words that have been uttered on this earth. God knows them all and has heard them all! AMAZING! The Glory and Power of our Lord is utterly amazing!

So, let's drop your jaw. God doesn't want us to be too smart. WHAT? I submit that God doesn't want to call people who know everything because a person, who is too intelligent, often will question things. When God calls you to do something, the last thing that he wants us to do is to question his call. If that is not freeing, I don't know what is. If you look at those God calls in the Bible, they are almost always everyday people, regular people. He usually doesn't call scholars; he usually doesn't call kings or queens. He calls those who are not even qualified to be a servant. You see, God does not call the qualified, He qualifies the called.

What if your dog was more intelligent than you? What if your dog could make more money than you or solve the family problems better than you? Would you still feed him? Would you still provide housing for him? How long before you just give the Family dog the keys to the house and say "lead me". . . . Your dog benefits from only knowing 100 words when related to a Master who knows 30,000 words. You are more intelligent than your dog, but give this thought . . . If you know 30,000 words and God knows septillion or octillions of words, are you ok with that? God wants to feed you; he wants you to lean on him. God wants you to look to him the way your family Dog looks to you for that which allows him to live. And sometimes, God just wants you to be a little dumb. WHAT? Let me rephrase that. Sometimes God just wants you to be dumb enough not to question him. Sometimes, God just wants you to listen instead of challenging him. Try it sometime. Let God take control of something small; it will give you so much freedom knowing that you are taken care of! Wow, that is good news!

We must also be careful about what we think that we know. You see, you can believe wholeheartedly that you can fly. However, if you jump out of an airplane without a parachute, you will, in all likelihood, die. The ground does not care that you thought you could fly. Gravity does not know that you believe that you are able to fly, when you can't. Just saying that something is true does not make it correct.

So, we must have a proven source of knowledge. Hmmm, I wonder what that could be? Well, the Bible, of course, has stood the test of time and stands as our rock in times of uncertainty. Cleave to it and let it be your guide. Don't make decisions based on your feelings; visit the scripture to guide your thoughts. And it is ok to be wrong if the Bible tells you that you are wrong. It is ok not to know much as long as you stand on the word of God. You don't need to know much of anything. Doesn't that make you feel free? Just trust in the word of God, follow that which the Bible tells you and there is no way that you will not be seen as holy and righteous in the eyes of God. It is a full-proof plan that requires no thought, just the act of saying, "I am not worthy, but I trust in your word God, guide me upon your path."

This makes me think of something that dogs do that often puzzles me. When you take a toy, shake it in front of a dog, and then throw the toy, your dog will almost always, without fail, run and get that toy. No matter what time of day it is, it becomes his job to fetch the toy you throw. It can be thought of as simple if you give it thought. You throw, the dog fetches. How simple that dog must be to do this every single time. But let's challenge you a little. Is this not what we humans do in our everyday lives? Someone throws that promotion, and we go and chase after it. We see a person that we are attracted to, and we chase after them. We see a beautifully engineered car, and we chase after it so that we can buy it. I imagine that it is often the case that when our dog gets to the toy, he must think to himself, "Wow, it isn't a real bone, it is just a toy". It is not going to bring me much joy, and so it becomes more about the hunt rather than the joy of the capture. As humans, I think that we also get what we are hunting too, and often we must feel the same as our dog in that we find out all too quickly that the very thing that we were searching or longing for isn't all that it is cracked up to be. And we find that it doesn't bring us much joy because it is not real. It is just a short-term glimpse of joy. And sometimes that which we strive toward only brings us grief when we thought the opposite of its capture. What if we taught ourselves to only seek that which brings true joy? If you believe in God and have Faith in God, why not trust him to be your joy? We can pin our happiness on the capture of things of this World, or we can pin our happiness on things outside of this World. It is not too hard to imagine that the love of Christ is eternal, and the Glory of God is everlasting, so if we pin our hunt upon these things, our joy will be endless as well. It takes time to learn this and implement it in your life, but if you seek to capture the Bible and his Word, you will find that Joy in there.

There are hundreds of scriptures in the Bible about seeking God, but my favorite is

Proverbs 8:17 "I love those who love me, and those who seek me find me."

It is so a matter of fact. Those who seek will find me. He is not hiding from you, he wants to be seen, and his promise is just that.

This brings to mind a cute little game that we eventually taught our dog, Max. I would go and hide in the house and Max would search for me. Our 'seek and find' game was a delight for us both. He loved searching (more like smelling his way to me) and I loved it when he found me and would give him "Good Boy" hugs! However, sometimes my hiding spot was too hard for him, and I had to call out his name "Max" or say "Help" just to give him the general direction. It put him back on the trail to help him find me again. God loves the same seek and find game! The difference is that God is not hiding, he is right out in the open and has open arms, and because of our sin, it is far too often that we just run right past him and do not even see him. Open your eyes . . . repent of your sin and seek him, and he will call your name out a few times until you find your way to him. Then you can get the hug of all hugs from God and the best "Atta boy" from the Almighty.

"Lord, help us all to find our way to you. Give us a gentle nudging to pinpoint the sin that we need to work on and give us a heading to you. We desire to know you and be in communion with you Lord. Thank you for the blessings that you have bestowed on us!"

You, God, and Your Dog

Chapter 7: What does a Dog Want?

Our little buddy Max had a little bit of separation anxiety. What he wanted most was to be with us, and it showed. Most Labradors are faithful dog companions, but Max was remarkable in that he would rather sit by your side or under your desk by your feet. When he reached 120 pounds, it was kind of hard to take him wanting to sit on your lap like a 10-pound tiny terrier. Yes, he reached 120 pounds. We put a camera in the living room so that we could see what he did when we left the house and found out that once we left, he would go to the front door, then back to the garage door, and then back to the front door over and over again. This repeated until we came home, and then he would flop down next to us and sleep. We had to work hard to give him comfort in knowing that we would always return, and with some work, he eventually learned that we would return to him when we briefly left the house. But that never changed that what he wanted most was to be at our side.

One day while my Wife and I were in a store, we saw a woman pushing a baby carriage and inside that carriage was her little dog. Her dog was not only being paraded around like royalty inside his very own carriage, but her dog was also dressed in the nicest little dog clothes. These clothes had rhinestones on them, and the fabric was all sparkly from also having stitched into it many sequins. The dog was being paraded around better than most children, yet he was just a dog. But to that lady who was his Owner, this dog was just like her child.

It got me thinking; does her dog want to be in this baby carriage all dressed up like royalty? If her dog was to choose how to spend his day, would he spend it getting all dressed up to impress? And if he could decide what to wear, or even wanted to have that choice, would he choose clothes with sparkly things sewn all over? My best guess is that if her dog had his way, he would not be wearing flashy clothes and would be most happy just sitting in a pile of mud rolling around getting all dirty.

But on that day, her dog was not rolling around in the mud. As the Master of that pet, this lady chose what the dog would wear and how the dog would be moving through the store. And as much as it was probably not part of what the dog would have wanted to be doing at that moment, he was doing exactly what his Master wanted him to do.

This made me think that often, we pray for specific things from God. We pray for money, we pray for a nice car or high-end clothes, we pray for a nice house, and the list goes on and on. Often, we pray for what we consider a need, and often, we feel that our prayers go unanswered. By the way, not getting an answer about prayer or not getting what we pray for is not an "unanswered" prayer. God does not need to qualify that he is not granting a wish, he just doesn't. God not providing what you want in life is also an answer, he just doesn't provide. Everything that we want, we don't always get . . . But everything that God wants, we get. His plan is more significant than your desires, so you can want things so badly, but you will not get it if it is not in his design for your life. Just like the dog who sits in a baby carriage being chauffeured around in a store. I would guess that this dog (if he prayed for things) would have prayed that same morning that he could just go to a mud hole, throw himself in, and have lots of fun. But the Master had a different plan that day and he had a sort of "doggy fashion day".

We are kind of like that too, don't you think? As humans, we often want to throw ourselves in the mud. We are carnal creatures, and we desire things of the flesh. We battle with our flesh every day. We battle with things of the World, and many times, we succumb to those things. We give in to the pleasures of the World and then find ourselves disconnected from our Lord. We pray for things that we feel will satisfy our desires, and then we get angry or disappointed when these carnal things do not come to us.

Being in the mud for a dog is just a physical act, and if you have ever had a dog full of dirt, you will know that the last place you want your pet to be is inside your house! And of course, the last place in your house that you want your pet is on your bed or couch! What has to happen before your dog comes into the house after playing in the mud all day long? They must be bathed and washed clean. It is much the same way with God and us. Being "in the mud" (sinning) for humans is repulsive to God. We somehow find pleasure in seeking and achieving carnal ways of drinking or doing drugs or whatever other carnal worldly things. God views us destroying our lives as us "playing in the mud", and before we can reconnect with him, we must be washed clean with a holy bath of sorts. When we succumb to sin and play in the mud, we become so dirty to God.

Galatians 5:18-21 says "Now the works of the flesh are evident: sexual immorality, impurity, sensuality, idolatry, sorcery, enmity, strife, jealousy, fits of anger, rivalries, dissensions, divisions, envy, drunkenness, orgies, and things like these. I warn you, as I warned you

before, that those who do such things will not inherit the kingdom of God."

Just like you don't want your dog to sit on your couch right after it has played in the mud all day, we also find ourselves in the position where God says no to us and wants us to be clean before coming into his house.

But let's go back to the little dog in the carriage. The pet inside the carriage does not know how to dress up like a king and be paraded around like royalty. But his Owner does. You see, when we pray for things that are not of God's will and we won't get answers or be given those things, but we get what God desires for our lives. And in return, we get dressed like a King, and we get paraded around like royalty! Isn't this excellent news? The dog in the carriage does not deserve to be treated like royalty, but his Master sees and cherishes him enough to treat him as such. The dog in the carriage does not desire to be prim and proper and be seen by others as beautiful, he just wants to play in the mud, but the Master has other plans.

Jeremiah 29:11 says: "For I know the plans I have for you, declares the Lord, plans for welfare and not for evil, to give you a future and a hope."

Sometimes, we must be willing just to let God do what is in his plans for our lives. Our job is to clean ourselves up, get rid of the mud and dirt on ourselves so that we can enter our Master's house. Once we get clean, we need to be ready to fight temptation and keep ourselves as clean as possible. By the way, don't be overly worried about actually "overcoming" sin . . . You cannot do it on your own. God knows that you cannot, and this is why he sent his Son. Jesus died for your inability to overcome sin. (Maybe not every day sins, but the original sin of his first creations). This original sin plagued humanity, and no matter what a person did, they could not clean the dirt and mud off enough to be presentable to God. So, God reset the World and gave us a chance to strive toward holiness and let Jesus take us the rest of the way to God.

The cool part of the correlation between that dog in the carriage and us is that once you clean off the mud and dirt in your life, God will dress you up like a king and parade you around like royalty. Just like the pet owner's dog, you are not worthy of such treatment, but the Master (God) wants it for you! This is such fantastic news! Our God loves and treasures us so much that he sees us as royalty when we are in his house, and he treats us as such too! We get the incredible chance to eat in his home and be surrounded by gemstones and the finest things of the Universe. We will be so content that all we will want to do is praise the God who provides. I get so excited when I think about the day when I will have the pleasure to praise a God who loves me enough to throw my sins as far as the East is from the West. What a glorious and righteous God we serve!

I do want to spend a few minutes making sure to clarify something. I have had dogs in the past that no matter how much teaching they received, nothing was learned. A few dogs we had were just not fit to live in our house with us. We had one dog named Tara, who defiantly dug a hole in the wall one day. Yes, this happened. I came home, and Tara had dug a two-foot hole in the drywall! Another day, she decided to just eat the rug; we had just replaced a rug because she could not learn to go outside for potty breaks. So as a result of this, we had to decide to build her a doghouse outside of our home, and she became an outside dog. This was not the original intent for her when we got her, but after years of not being able to train her how to behave inside our home, we had to make the tough decision to restructure her living situation to outside. When we wash off the dirt and sin from our life, by accepting Jesus as our Lord and Savior, we are welcome into God's house. But what happens when we do not leave sin behind? What happens when we continue to live a life filled with sin? God allows us to live in sin as we all have the choice to make that decision. However, God cannot turn a blind eye to sin, and he cannot allow you to be in his house while you are sinning. Jesus said in

Matthew 10:14: "If anyone will not welcome you or listen to your words, leave that home or town and shake the dust off your feet."

During the days when the Bible was written, when a Jew left a city where unbelievers lived, they would often shake the dust from their feet to signify disapproval of the practices of the people of that town. If the disciples shook the dust from their feet after leaving a town where Jews lived, it would show their disapproval of Jews who did not accept Jesus. This means that if you tell someone about God and they reject you and continue to sin, you have done your part, and you should wipe off your feet and move on and separate yourself from their sinful life. If Jesus said this, then I venture to believe that even God gets to a point where he "lets us go". God does not want you to be a holy prisoner; he wants you to be holy because you want to be holy and desire to be closer to him. You cannot become white as snow without the help of Jesus' sacrifice, but you can undoubtedly strive toward holiness. And if you come to know God and accept Christ as your Lord and Savior but continue to live in sin, you are pressing the boundaries of God's ability to allow you to be in his house.

Just like my dog Tara, do not be so bad and displeasing to God that he puts you outside of his house! You do not have to be perfect, but if you make an effort, and God sees that effort, he will close the gap for you! As written above, he loves you enough to forgive your sins if you repent and turn from them; Just like Jesus did for the woman caught in adultery. In the Gospel of John, Chapter 8, there is a story of a woman caught in the act of adultery. In those days, people would stone the woman to death due to her act of adultery. In the account of that day's event, Jesus took the time to stop them from stoning her and said one of the most memorable phrases in the Bible.

John 8:7 "Let anyone of you that is without sin, cast the first stone at her"

Jesus taught a few lessons on that day in

passing judgment on others while sinning yourself. But an equally important lesson is that he did not condemn the woman to be stoned for her sin; he told her to stand up and move forward. But and this is especially important; he ends his time with her by saying, "sin no more". So, her sins were forgiven, and she was saved from death; however, with that came the responsibility of moving forward and not committing the sin again. I interpret his actions that day as motivation to know that you are forgiven but to also strive toward goodness. If you get to know God, your desire should change as well. You will transform from a carnal creature to one of structure, discipline, and holiness.

I wish it were always as easy as saying, "Don't play in the mud," but maybe it is? You have a lifetime to decide that. A lifetime no matter how short or long it is to live in preparation to live like royalty in the house of the King! Let God's will be done and let his face shine upon us!

Chapter 8: Community

Have you ever noticed that even though your dog loves you so much and is happy to be with you, he is most comfortable with other dogs? When a dog is with other dogs, they enjoy running around after each other and just enjoying the company of another dog companion. They recognize each other as old friends, and even if they have just met, they quickly get over being shy and start to treat each other like old friends.

We are called to be the same way. God has built into us a wanting for Community. Many people think that God is their personal God, and this is somewhat true in that God knows every hair on your head and everything intimate about you and your life. However, God wants us to be in Community with others.

Philippians 2:3-4 says "Do nothing out of selfish ambition or vain conceit. Rather, in humility value others above yourselves, not looking to your own interests but each of you to the interests of the others."

If you place others' needs as valuable, it will fill something inside of you, and you will feel the same joy that your dog does when they are with other pets. God desires us to be looking outward and not inward. We are most fulfilled when we seek to take care of others and not dwell on our needs. If you dwell on your needs or things that you do not have or something that you want, it often makes you depressed and sad. God does not want you to be depressed and sad.

When we spend time with others, we start to feel the exact needs of others. There begins to be a common union between you and other Christ believers. Your conversations will always steer toward Christ. What you speak and what you do will start to steer toward the goodness of the Gospel and away from the ways of the World. This Common Union between you and other Christians will only uplift you. And once you start to see value in being with others, you will begin to eat with them and spend time with them just spending time together. This 'common union' begins to develop into Communion.

When he was at the last supper, Christ shared communion with his disciples. He broke bread with them and drank with them. This was so powerful because he taught them and us the power of being with other believers. He said in

Matthew 26:26 "Take this bread
and eat it, this is my body"

When you consume 'all things Jesus', you begin to be transformed into what Christ wants for you. And when you have communion with others and begin to consume Jesus together, it takes on an extraordinary feeling.

So just like your pet dog loves to be around other dogs, make sure to take time to break bread with other believers. God must smile every time we sit with friends and speak his name. God delights in our happiness, so make sure to be happy!

56

Chapter 9: You are your Dog's Master

There is nothing better than training your dog to walk calmly next to you so that the leash is not being pulled. I see so many people walking dogs, however it is the dog who is walking them. One of the things that I taught our little Max was to heel. It took many hours for him to learn that what I wanted was for him to not pull on the leash and to stay on my side and walk at the same pace as I am. Let me tell you that when he gets it right, it is a beautiful thing. He is my loving pet, and I am his Master. He does what I want him to do, and in turn, it makes both of our lives better. I do not look like a fool struggling with my out-of-control animal, and he is safe by my side.

God wants to be your Master. And just like you hugging and loving on your dog, God wants to be your best friend too. Just like you love being with your cute dog, God enjoys being with you!

**1 Timothy 2:3-4. "This is good,
and pleases God our Savior, who
wants all people to be saved and to
come to the knowledge of the truth"**

So let me ask you. Do you think that you will be able to train a dog even it is deemed untrainable? I submit that your dog must be somewhat trainable for you to teach him much. There are some dogs that even professional trainers cannot train. And no matter how hard someone tries; the dog just does not get it. Your dog must want to please you and, in doing so, is trainable. I firmly believe that. Do not worry; I also believe that you must also be a good trainer; the dog becomes a trained dog by wanting to please you. This is the canvas that we must be for God as well. He can often train us with ease if we simply want to please God. When we are stubborn and untrainable, God must allow us to learn the lesson the hard way.

I do not know about you, but my life is riddled with so many struggles that I have to admit are entirely because of my stubbornness. If I could have fully given in to the teaching of the Lord earlier in life, I am confident that I could (just like my dog does with me) walk side by side with the Lord and calmly go where he wants me to go. And when we are done walking where my Lord wants to go, I get the pleasure of spending time with him just letting him take care of me, love on me and be my friend!

2 Chronicles 7:17 "As for you, if you faithfully follow me as David your father did, obeying all my commands, decrees, and regulations, then I will establish the throne of your dynasty."

WOW . . . THAT is amazing to realize the simplicity of this exercise of walking with God. All you need to do is want to please him and allow him to guide you and not be stubborn about wanting to go your way. So why do we make it so hard?

There are so many times that we catch our pet just sitting and staring at us as dog owners. Why do they do that? I submit that they are looking for us to give them a command, but I also leave the possibility of them just admiring us as well. Your dog waits on your every word, they wait to hear what you have to say and yearn to understand the words you speak to them. Isn't this an excellent model for how we are to treat God . . . Our Bibles? If we act the same way that our dog acts toward us and we focus on God, and we strive to hear his command, we are in the right place to not only understand what it is that he is saying to us but accept it as his will for us and not ours.

Psalm 119:105 "Your word is a lamp to my feet and a light to my path."

When you finally make a statement to your pet and tell them to sit, they do it, right? So, as you practice to be more attentive to what God is trying to say to you, make sure to also practice how to do what he says . . . What he says should be acted upon without hesitation. It does free up your mind for just serving and not figuring things out.

1 Kings 2:3 "Observe what the LORD your God requires: Walk in obedience to him, and keep his decrees and commands, his laws and regulations, as written in the Law of Moses. Do this so that you may prosper in all you do and wherever you go."

So, this leads us to the question of how do we know what God is saying? That is such a great question. I submit that the first time you give a command to your new pet dog, he has no idea what you are saying. He wags his tail and comes to you with glee that he has heard your voice, and he believes that you are talking to him. It takes weeks, if not months, for your dog to understand even the simplest of commands. So how does he reach the point of actually knowing what you want of him? Repetition, that is how. The more you say a word and teach how to respond to that word, the more that our dog knows what we want of him. It truly is a learned behavior, and understanding and hearing from God is just as dependent on being a learned behavior. When we say to others that "I don't hear from God", we are saying that we have not learned how to hear from God.

Luke 11:28 "But he said, "Blessed rather are those who hear the word of God and keep it!"

Romans 10:17 "So faith comes from hearing, and hearing through the word of Christ."

To start the process of hearing from God we must know where to begin the learning process. We can stare at God all that we want, and he desires to speak to us, but we cannot understand the words he says, just like our new puppy. So, the rule is to read your Bible, meditate on the words in it, and let them marinate in your heart. The repetitive necessity of this action will allow your head to start to understand what your heart and ears hear from

God. And here is where the repetition comes into play. You must read and re-read some things many times to begin to understand the voice of God. His voice and the meaning of what he says are entirely different than what we think is rightful commands. Once your heart is willing to accept the voice of God, it will be at that time that you hear what he is saying. The words within the Bible will begin to speak directly to you; they will, in effect, become the voice of God. It takes much practice to see how God speaks to you, but just like our loving pets, we are to continually stare and fixate on our God and practice hearing his command. Then one day, we do it right. From that point, it will become a matter of habit; God will be speaking to you every day!

John 10:27 "My sheep hear my voice, and I know them, and they follow me."

We have all experienced that even though our dog knows what we are saying, it is very apparent that he does not want to do it. I can attest that what God has to say will not always be what you want to hear, and we will begrudgingly walk around in circles in defiance of his word.

Romans 8:7 "For the mind that is set on the flesh is hostile to God, for it

does not submit to God's law; indeed, it cannot."

God will repeat it and with a little more force. If we do not follow the command, there is a reprimand which will come soon. God does not want to hurt us, but he does want us to learn. And just like anything in life, we sometimes learn by failing. The beauty of this as it pertains to your dog is that even when our loving pet does not do what we ask of him, we still love him, so too does God. But so much so that he sends his Son to die on the cross for us. So, no matter how much grace we think that we give to our cute little puppy, who has chewed up the leg on the couch, it pales in comparison to the grace we receive from above. God is infinitely loving!

2 Corinthians 12:9 "But he said to me, "My grace is sufficient for you, for my power is made perfect in weakness." Therefore, I will boast all the more gladly of my weaknesses, so that the power of Christ may rest upon me."

So lastly, with the words of "God is infinitely loving" comes the reality of our relationship with

God. Yes, God is infinitely loving, but he is also infinitely able to rebuke as well. I submit that Jesus came to die on the cross for the sins of all mankind, not just yours. Jesus dying gives us the head start at life to not be saddled with original sin. He has removed it. We do not enter Heaven through works, but let's not be naïve in thinking that what we do and how we do it does not affect our relationship with God. God will rebuke you; God will reprimand you. He does this not to be mean to us but to teach us. If we are wise, we learn from these times of rebuke and live better. But if we do not learn and continue to live a sinful life, we are in peril of separation from God.

I had a dog once who was awful . . . I got so tired of him chewing everything, peeing everywhere, eating the wall (yes, I said it), digging up the carpets, and being an awful part of the house, that we gave him away. He was untrainable. It is essential to understand that separation from God removes you from being a part of the family as well. And just like the horrible dog that I had; you will be let go. I do not submit to the notion of "Once saved, always saved". I believe that if you ask for forgiveness, God forgives you and accepts you into his fold in the blink of an eye. But with becoming a part of the Family of God comes responsibility. You must strive to be a better Christian and try your best to live a sinless life. You must continually strive to be a better person in the eyes of God. I am not talking about flippant sins, but sins that are willfully done with you knowing that they are wrong. I believe that all sin is equally as bad for us, but I also believe that willful sin is attached to that which we have in our hearts. God knows what is in your heart, which means he knows which sin is committed by mistake and which is done deliberately. When you commit deliberate or willful sin, you are essentially telling God that you do not care. Deliberate and unrepented sin will separate you from God and his plan for your life. So, know that rebuke is a good thing, but 'act' afterward.

God has infinite grace, lean on that, let it be a crutch for you . . . but do not find yourself living in willful sin as it leads a rational thought to wonder if you were ever Christian in the first place.

Jeremiah 32:17-25 "Dear God, my Master, you created earth and sky by your great power by merely stretching out your arm! There is nothing you can't do. You're loyal in your steadfast love to thousands upon thousands, but you also make children live with the fallout from their parents' sins. Great and powerful God, named God-of-the-

Angel-Armies, determined in purpose and relentless in following through, you see everything that men and women do and respond appropriately to the way they live, to the things they do. You performed signs and wonders in the country of Egypt and continue to do so right into the present, right here in Israel and everywhere else, too. You've made a reputation for yourself that doesn't diminish. You brought your people Israel out of Egypt with signs and wonders a powerful deliverance, by merely stretching out your arm. You gave them this land and solemnly promised to their ancestors a bountiful and fertile land. But when they entered the land and took it over, they didn't listen to you. They didn't do what you commanded. They wouldn't listen to a thing you told them. And so you brought this disaster on them. Oh, look at the siege ramps already set in place to take the

city. Killing and starvation and disease are on our doorstep. The Babylonians are attacking! The Word you spoke is coming to pass it's daily news! And yet you, God, the Master, even though it is certain that the city will be turned over to the Babylonians, also told me, buy the field. Pay for it in cash. And make sure there are witnesses.'

Let God be your Master? Hmmm . . . Let that sink in. A servant does not question the Master; they just do. And if they do not, there is a consequence of not obeying. Our lives and how we live are artfully created within the confines of us being the servant and God being the Master. We must take this time on Earth to learn to hear his voice and act on the words he says while staying close to him with how we live. It is essential to lead a purpose-driven good life that is pleasing to God. This will not determine our entrance into Heaven but will prove our loyalty to God and his design. And when we see him face to face, he will know our name and be ready for us when we arrive.

Lord, please direct our path to where you want us to go. Show us your grace while giving us your loving touch in the right direction. Allow us to hear you. We seek to be a part of your family and have peace that you will know us as we return home to you. Thank you, Lord, for teaching us what it is to understand you and be a part of your family every day. And although we are not worthy, we thank you for the grace you give to us.

Chapter 10: Family

Maybe a few do not, but most of us consider our furry dog a part of the family. I hope that I am not the only one? We call them our little boy or precious girl, and when we refer to ourselves when talking to the dog, most of us call ourselves Mommy and Daddy. They sleep in our bed, they sit with us while we watch television, and they are at our feet when we cook in the kitchen. They are as much a part of our family as even our children. And yet, let's give this thought. We accept them into our family even given the apparent reality that they seriously do not fit there. They are hairy; oh the hair, let it stop, please! They smell awful at times, ok, ok, almost all the time. They don't share food with anyone. They don't provide or work to bring money in for the household. They don't do the laundry or clean up after themselves, yet we treat them as a necessary part of our family.

If you give it thought, without any emotion, the choice to consider your dog as part of your family is kind of ridiculous. And yet we do. We feed them without asking for anything in return. We give them shelter, a bed, toys, and safety, and we ask nothing from them in return. They get a free pass on really not doing much of anything. All we ask of our dog is to behave.

Isaiah 40:28 "Have you not known? Have you not heard? The Lord is the everlasting God, the Creator of the ends of the earth. He does not faint or grow weary; his understanding is unsearchable"

So too is it for God. If you think about the omnipotence of God, it is hard to imagine that even though we were created in his image, we are not anywhere close to the likeness of God. (As it pertains to the lives we lead on this Earth) In comparison to God, we must be like mongrels nipping at his feet just to get a bite to eat. Many of us do nothing to help Heaven, and yet God provides for us, and he watches over us. On the face of it, we are sinners who don't have any place inside the Family of God, and yet he yearns for us to love and fellowship with him, and his hands are outstretched, waiting for us at all times. God does not ask much of us in offering his love and support. God loves us even though we are the most unlikely member of the Family of God, being him and the Angels.

1 John 1:6-7 "If we say that we have fellowship with Him, and walk in darkness, we lie and do not practice the truth. But if we walk in the light as He is in the light, we have fellowship with one another, and the blood of Jesus Christ His Son cleanses us from all sin."

God does not ask us to pay any of Heaven's bills; he does not ask us to pay for food, keep Heaven clean, or do any of the chores that a Family does. Just as it is with our meager expectation for our dog, all God asks us to do is to behave. God merely wants us to strive for holiness, not for his benefit but ours. Hopefully, along the way, we begin to learn how to praise our Master.

As a dog owner, I do not expect much from my puppy. It works to his benefit to be too cute for me to banish him from the house when he makes a mistake on my new carpet. And they do . . . But then something begins to happen as a dog grows. They "learn" to be a part of our family. We accept them first, and then they learn to be a part. It takes years and years for a dog to show how worthy they are to be considered a part of the family. In those years, they learn to be warriors at the front door; they learn to take it outside when they have to go, they learn to be with us when we are sorrowful, they learn to bring us a toy when they feel that we need to play and they learn to . . . behave. THIS is what we ultimately want from our dog, to behave, and once our dog learns this, we can fully enjoy our pet being a part of our family.

John 1:12 "But to all who did receive him, who believed in his name, he gave the right to become children of God"

What if we could just learn this about God? Striving to be holy is what makes you truly a part of God's Family. At first, God does not ask anything of us but to just be baby Christians, and then a little more and a little more. And then one day, years and years later, he looks at us and says, "Good and Faithful servant," and then he can fully enjoy us being a part of his family. The highly unlikely and sinful people we are who once should never have been allowed to be in the Family of God are now looking like possibly, a likely Son or Daughter of the King. How blessed are we that we have a God who has his arms open wide at every moment of the day even though we do not deserve his loving grace? Even though, in reality, I should not be a part of his extraordinary and everlasting household because of my sinful ways, I am still considered a part and allowed to grow into it. It takes years and years for our dog to learn to be a part of our family and for us, it is just the same.

The learning process for a dog can be rough along the way, but when it all turns out right, we revel in what a great animal we have and how well pleased we are in him. All that matters in life is that God looks at us in the same way. All I desire in life is for God to look at me and know that I love him and that I am his servant and pray that I become worthy enough to sit at his table. And hopefully, hear him call me . . . his family.

You, God, and Your Dog

Chapter 11: Man's Best Friend

Max had the most wonderful ability to make you feel special. When you were with him, you just knew that you were his World. When I was a young boy, I would play for hours with my friends on the street. We would throw a ball back and forth or kick the soccer ball up and down the road together. We would grab our fishing poles, head over the canal, and try to catch fish. It was these activities that made them what I considered a friend. Max did those same things. He loved to play ball, and pulling on a rope was one of his favorites. It meant as much to me playing those games as it did to him. He truly was a friend indeed.

Why did God create us? When in the very first chapter of the Bible it says,

Genesis 1:27 "So God created man in his own image, in the image of God he created them, male and female"

What is the point? The point resoundingly is that we are to be a mirror reflection of God. And when taken in context with

Isaiah 43:6-7 "I will say to the north, 'Give them up!' and to the south, 'Do not hold them back.' Bring my sons from afar and my daughters from the ends of the earth. Everyone who is called by my name, whom I created for my glory, whom I formed and made."

It is clear that the reflection is to bring glory to God. How powerful is it that we as humans were designed, created, and exist for the glory of our creator, and how freeing is it that our existence is to complete that glory? The only thing that we have to attain in our lives is learning to love God with our whole hearts. The only thing that we have to achieve in our life is to be worthy of bringing him glory. WOW, I don't know about you, but bringing God glory IS our reward, and if that is the reward for eternity, how gratifying do you think it will be? I imagine it to be abundantly and infinitely gratifying, as the Bible states in

Revelation 21:4 that "He will wipe away every tear from their eyes, and

death shall be no more, neither shall there be mourning, nor crying, nor pain, for the former things, have passed away."

This promise tells me that our eternity in Heaven will be one without any cause for fear or sorrow. And where there is one full positive, there can be no negative, so there must transversely be all positive where there is no negative.

So, I expect that Heaven will be fully and infinitely enjoyable and that it will be filled with glory to God, so in turn, giving glory to God will be fully and infinitely rewarding . . . for eternity.

When we see our dog, there are not too many people who don't view that little guy as their best friend. It is universally accepted that dogs are man's best friend, and there is a reason for that. When your dog looks at you, believe it or not, he is trying desperately to tell you that he is here for you, that he is ready to serve you. There is nothing that your dog won't do for you and the very last question that he would ask, (if he could ask a question), would be "Why?" He just does it. His whole life is to serve you as his Master. That is such a great comparison of how we are to be to our Heavenly Father . . . We shouldn't ask "Why" when we are told to do something, we should just follow the command and do it. In my opinion, THIS is what we are here on Earth to learn. We are here to learn how to be like our dogs. We are here to learn how to do everything we do to bring glory to our Master. And when your dog does something correctly, he is so proud, he is so happy. So, we are also here to learn that bringing glory to God also brings happiness to us; the kind of happiness that we can only get by doing so.

How beautiful it is to know that serving our creator will complete us. That is all it is about. And like our lovely pets, we, in return, will receive fulfillment beyond what we could otherwise achieve as a dog's purpose is to be man's best friend, but only so much as it relates to what he does for us, not because of what we give to the dog. WOW, that is an excellent theology. Our dog "Asks not what we can do for him, but what he can do for us," and we should, in turn, be asking God what we can do for him and not what he can do for us. This is the meaning of life, learn this and believe in God and Eternity with the creator is yours, as is the happiness and fulfillment that comes along with it as being "God's best friend."

Chapter 12: GOOD BOY

One of the very first words that my dog heard from me was, "You're a good boy!" And when he did something correctly, the "You're a good boy" got an elevated voice and tons of loving hugs too. You tell your dog to "come" and when they do for the first time, you praise them with "Good Boy!" You tell your dog to "Let go of the toy" and when they do, you say "Good Boy!". It is this affirmation that they come to yearn for and desire! The encouragement of that moment is the most essential aspect of his time with me. And so, this phrase turns out to be the one phrase that almost all dogs wag their tail when they hear.

How much does your dog love to hear these words? A LOT. Sometimes it is all they live to hear. Well, except for "Do you want to go for a ride in the car?", or "Do you want to eat". When your dog hears words of encouragement, it isn't hard to see how much he loves it. That wagging tail and excited hopping around speaks volumes about his feeling of joy.

God is encouraging.

Jeremiah 29:11 "For I know the plans I have for you, declares the Lord, plans to prosper you and not harm you, plans to give you hope and a future"

We exist to praise the Lord. The entirety of who we are, what we do, and why we are here is to learn to glorify God. Our lives on this Earth are 80, 90, or 100 years of practice in total devotion to God. And with that being said, isn't it wonderful that even though it is not about us but rather about the living God, that same God showers us with love and hope? God wants us to feel his love. It is important to him that we are in communion with him and that we feel worthy to be in his presence. Of course, we are not worthy, but isn't it nice that he desires us to think as such? What a truly loving God who wants this for us. This should be on every person's prayer each day to say the words "I am not worthy, but thank you Lord for giving me hope in you that I have worth in all things." Imagine how beautiful it must be to be in total devotion to God so much so that we don't need to accomplish anything in Heaven.

Just praising God will fill our hearts with more than we can imagine, and there will be no regrets as we do it. This is hard to imagine, isn't it? But it is accurate. God waits for us to be spiritually grown enough to set aside our thinking and replace it with his. And one day, when we have passed from this World, we will get the honor of just being near to him. It is not farfetched that being near him will instantaneously spur our voices to proclaim him King and praise his holy name for the rest of Eternity. THAT is powerful; that is Love, acceptance, and an eternity that I long for. How about you?

You, God, and Your Dog

Chapter 13: BAD BOY

So far too often, we spend the first few years of our dog's life "reminding" them that they have done something bad. Max has decided to go inside the house . . . BAD BOY! Max has decided to eat the baseboard . . . BAD BOY! Max has decided to chew at the table leg . . . BAD BOY! Max just got done rummaging through the garbage . . . BAD BOY! And the list goes on and on.

So, this brings to mind, why we do this. Why do we consistently say "Bad Boy" to our dog when he does something terrible? Is it to make him feel bad? Is it to put him in his place or make him feel less important to us? Of course not. It is so that he knows that we want something different from him. And if we say it enough, it is the hope that eventually he will stop doing the negative activity and give us reasons to praise him.

Hebrews 4:9-13 "There remains, then, a Sabbath-rest for the people of God; for anyone who enters God's rest also rests from their works, just as God did from his. Let us, therefore, make every effort to enter

that rest, so that no one will perish by following their example of disobedience."

For the word of God is alive and active. Sharper than any double-edged sword, it penetrates even to dividing soul and spirit, joints and marrow; it judges the thoughts and attitudes of the heart. Nothing in all of creation is hidden from God's sight. Everything is seen and revealed before the eyes of God to whom we must give account.

Please take the time to re-read this . . .

The Bible gives us all knowledge about what we need to know in distinguishing the difference between genuinely selfless, spiritual deeds and acts that are selfish and ungodly. Even Jesus describes how the Pharisees' behavior in and of itself is not always obedience in Mathew 23 when he gave a warning to the hypocrisy of teachers of the law and of the Pharisees.

It is possible to read the Bible and yet not understand or follow God's true will due to the rebellion inside of our hearts.

2 Peter 3:16 He writes the same way in all his letters, speaking in them of these matters. His letters contain some things that are hard to understand, which ignorant and unstable people distort, as they do the other Scriptures, to their own destruction."

The context of Hebrews 4:9-13 is crucial. Verse 11 warns us to attempt to obey God, or we lose our heavenly rewards. In verse 12 we learn that the Bible gives us the ability to understand the true will of God. And in verse 13 we find that God's judgment is inevitable: No person is beyond his knowledge; he knows all.

2 Corinthians 5:10, ESV: "For we must all appear before the judgment seat of Christ, so that each one may receive what is due for what he has done in the body, whether good or evil." We will each receive whatever we deserve for the good or evil we have done in this earthly body."

And isn't it good news to have grace through our Lord Jesus Christ, in that only in Christ do we find a God who truly understands our failures.

Hebrews 4:14-16 "Therefore, since we have a great high priest who has ascended into heaven, Jesus the Son of God, let us hold firmly to the faith we profess. For we do not have a high priest who is unable to empathize with our weaknesses, but we have one who has been tempted in every way, just as we are yet he did not sin. Let us then approach God's throne of grace with confidence, so that we may receive mercy and find grace to help us in our time of need."

So, when God says, "BAD BOY", it is one of the greatest opportunities that we have. It is our chance to correct. This loving rebuke affords us the ability to be closer to him because if we are sinning, God cannot be near us. Sin separates us from God and if we willfully sin in our lives, we ultimately choose to separate ourselves from God. It is the lucky ones who hear the "BAD BOY!" words from God and decide to do something about it. Given the willingness on our part to allow for correction from the words within the Bible, we can free ourselves from the bondage of sin. You see, Jesus died so that we can live by way of his sacrifice, giving us cover to the sin in our lives, and this is the crutch that we need to make it to Heaven. But . . . and this is a big but . . . we should not plan on using this sacrifice as an unneeded crutch either.

The worst thing that you can do, and what probably grieves the Spirit more than you can imagine, is to continue to sin knowing that you are sinning and using the sacrifice of Jesus so that you can "continue to sin". I would think that God sees this as a form of apostasy. For, if you minimalize the sacrifice of Jesus (to turn it into gain so that you can live a sinful lifestyle), you are in total rejection of God. And reject the true reason for our existence.

2 Peter 2:20-22 "For if, after they have escaped the defilements of the world through the knowledge of our Lord and Savior Jesus Christ, they are again entangled in them and overcome, the last state has become worse for them than the first. For it would have been better for them never to have known the way of righteousness than after knowing it to

**turn back from the holy
commandment delivered to them.
What the true proverb says has
happened to them: The dog returns
to its own vomit, and the sow, after
washing herself, returns to wallow in
the mire."**

When God rebukes us, it is his way of showing his love for us. Just like we scold our furry little friend so that he can find a good fit inside of our family, so too does God rebuke us so that he can be in communion with us. What a wonderful promise that God has cleared for us! He knows that he cannot be around sin, yet he desires to be near to us. He knows that he cannot just turn a blind eye to our sin, so he gave us the "ability" to make it to Heaven through Jesus; all while expecting us to act to keep our lives in harmony with his law. If we act, the sacrifice takes us the rest of the way there, and we are no longer held in bondage by sin.

**Romans 5:8 "God loves us even
when we make mistakes. But God
demonstrates his own love toward us,**

in that while we were still sinners, Christ died for us"

This was one of the most complex things for me to learn in my own life. And is this next understanding that gives me hope but also checks my spirit to be better at being Holy. So many people have been taught that your works here on Earth will earn you a place in Heaven, and only by those works can you make it to Heaven. Some people also believe that no matter what you do on this Earth you will always have a seat with the King if you only confess that you are a believer. I believe that the truth is somewhere in the middle of that. I believe that we are born sinners; we cannot save ourselves and make it to Heaven no matter how hard we try. I thank God every day that he has given me the chance to be redeemed through the blood of Christ. But I also believe that we must ACT. We must strive to be Holy; we must attempt to be Holy, we must examine our lives in every way and every day so that we can be closer to whom Jesus was on this Earth. If we act and strive to be better, no sin separates us from God.

Isaiah 1:18 says, "Come now, let us reason together, says the Lord. Though your sins are like scarlet, they shall be as white as snow."

So, I submit to you today that hearing the gentle nudge from God is one of the most beautiful things that you will hear. Open your heart and let him in. Give yourself to him and let his will be yours. Die to yourself and follow. God is waiting to be with you here on Earth and in Heaven. It is his promise.

Chapter 14: Conclusion

I know that some of the readers of this book will think that I am trying to compare humans to dogs. In attempting to assure you that I am not doing this, I want to share how the idea of this book came about. My wife and I have a few grandchildren. One day, one of the girls drew us a picture after getting home from Church. She told us that it was God, and she made the drawing of him with a crown on his head. She wrote what was supposed to be the word "God" next to him, but because she was only five at the time, she spelled it as "doG". I don't know exactly why, but when I saw this, I immediately began to formulate in my mind "GOD/DOG" and was immediately filled with ways to interact with our pets and how similar it is to our relationship with them God. I would be sleeping and wake up and write down what I heard God saying to me on a notepaper. I can genuinely say that I felt God lead me as I wrote the words in this book. So I want to assure all those who read this book that I am not comparing us to dogs; we are Sons and Daughters of the King.

We do not grovel at the feet of the King; we are mighty warriors. However, we should not fill our minds with being so significant that we put God in a box. We are here for God and not the other way around. We are here to serve God and not the other way around. This book is not written to minimize us, instead it is written to encourage us that even though we are not worthy, God wants and pursues us. I hope that after reading this, it is seen as a lighthearted approach to becoming a part of the Family of God.

Your journey toward God is much like a mountain. God is at the top of the mountain, and the journey to him will lead you from the bottom to the very top. Getting there takes a lifetime. Your lifetime might be short or long. But we are all guaranteed to die, and this unknown is the journey. So, when does your journey to God begin? I submit that the first step to climbing that mountain is to accept Christ as your Lord and Savior.

The first step you take toward God on that mountain starts with dying to yourself and humbly giving your life over to God through Jesus. You see, Christ died for the sins of mankind, not so that you can sin! Maybe our view of Heaven is above us and Hell being below us is more of a perfect way of the journey than we have ever thought about? You see, falling into a pit requires minimal effort. All you need to do is fall. Gravity takes over from there, and the journey down requires so little effort. Those who fall away from God do not need to do anything other than let gravity take its course. And in not acting, we will simply fall until we hit rock bottom and find ourselves in Hell. There is no return trip from that location. Then there is the journey up the mountain to God. The first step is to accept Christ, but the rest of the journey is tough. Have you ever climbed a mountain? It requires willpower, commitment, and resolve. It requires planning and thought. One does not just start climbing a mountain and take a few steps to reach the top. The greatest mountain climbers will tell you that most will fail, and only those who made the clear choice to reach the top will succeed. The journey will be arduous, exhaustive, challenging, and at times more than we think that we can bear.

The road to God up that mountain is so hard that many will not make it to the top. And when we have broken our leg when we sin, Jesus offers us a crutch of his sacrifice. But having that crutch does not mean that we do not have to continue to walk. It makes the journey possible, not easier. The journey to the top of that mountain will take you a lifetime. Wouldn't it be great if you made such a commitment in your life that you know beyond a shadow of a doubt that when your time is ended on Earth, you will have reached the top of the mountain to God? Jesus has promised it to us, and if we commit ourselves to holiness and continual self-reflection, we are assured of the summit!

Praise God!

Isn't it funny what most people think about death? (The top of the mountain) They see death as a scary event. Most likely, this is because, to many, there is ultimately an unknown about what happens when you close your eyes for the final time here on Earth. I know so many Christians who are really strong believers and, yet fear death. We spend so much time going to Church and growing in our Faith, but we then desperately clutch so tightly onto the few moments we have on Earth. Having a firm belief of where you will go after death is so freeing. And in a moment, your eyes will close and reopen to meet Jesus face to face. I don't know about you, but that is the most exciting thing I can imagine. What will that moment be like?

Peace to you all, and do not forget to live with a purpose that follows God's plan for you. And just like our little furry buddies . . . Don't forget to every now and then, just lie at his feet and enjoy his presence!

Chapter 15: Euthanasia

During the writing of this book, my wife and I find ourselves having to make the incredibly tough decision to put our wonderful dog, Max to sleep. It has been months of us discussing when the time will be right. He is almost 12 and suffers from many dog-related ailments which prohibit him from enjoying life to the fullest. However, the more serious issues like having a hard time breathing or walking in discomfort forced us to make that tough decision.

This got me thinking about finishing this book.

Suppose the premise of this book is to outline the similarities of our dog's relationship to us and our relationship to God. Can I make a comparison of Euthanasia as well? My thoughts bring me to the age-old question of "Why did God allow this to happen in my life?" or "Why did God allow this good person to die?" These questions will often cause a person to stray from their path to God. Often, a hardship or heartache will cause us to abandon God because we think he does not care about us enough to stop the bad things from happening.

So what is the reason for us putting our awesome friend to sleep? Why are we even considering it? The answer is a tough one and the decision has been seemingly impossible. But in my heart, I believe that we are making this decision for Max for his good. It is so that he does not have to endure the pain anymore. It is because I am smarter than my pet, and I know that his hips will not get better but worse. I don't know the future for my loving pet, but I do know the probable outcome, which includes him suffering. So when God says "No" to one of my prayers, I have to also believe that he is smarter than I am. I have to believe that he has my best interest at heart. When God does not step in to save a dying person, we need to know that God knows the probable outcome of that person's life. Maybe life would have been more than his Child could take? It is up to us not to question why God does something or allows something but to know in our hearts that God is in control. He is the author of life, and we are to put our lives in his hands fully. Much like Max allows me to feed him and take care of him, he also has to allow me to decide even about the end of his life.

Max will remain in our hearts for the rest of our lives. I will forever remember all of the days of love that he has given to us. But after writing this book, I will remember how he taught me a more important lesson - The comparison of his relationship with me and how closely that resembles my relationship with God. When my time comes to leave this World, I want God to say, "Good Boy" and I want to not only be inside of his heart for eternity but have the ultimate pleasure of basking in his Glory for the rest of days. All praise and power to our wonderful God, who is all-knowing and all-powerful.

Wink . . . Wink to my Max. Thank you, my faithful friend!

Chapter 16: Our Max

To whoever knew him, they know what a gentle giant he was! Twelve years of friendship put on brief hold as our wonderful dog makes his final trip to the Vet. I say brief hold because it has to be true that pets such as this with such a special bond will follow us to the life after this. This will be the first time he goes with us in the car that I will not ask him, "Do you want to go for a ride?" It is heartbreaking.

Max joyfully stayed at our side every moment of his life, and his loyalty showed in that he constantly gazed into our eyes to tell us that he loved us. His eyes were as deep as his heart, and when he looked at us, it was as if he was letting us know the pure nature of his love. He solely relied on us, and he taught me how I should interact with my Master, Our Lord God.

I can honestly say to Max on his last day on Earth - "Thank you, you were a good and faithful servant."

. . . And I strive to hear the same from our Father in Heaven when the time comes for me to meet him.

Max, Black Labrador Retriever 2009-2021

You, God, and Your Dog

About the Author:

A Son, Husband, Father, Brother, and Pop (Grandfather). I love being all of these. Life without one of these titles would not seem normal. My wife is the light of my life, and my children make me so proud. The grandchildren that I have are precious gifts, and I look forward to having the chance to spend more time with even more of them as time goes by.

I want all who read this book to know that I am an average person with many faults. I struggle daily with the same challenges as everyone. I question God and the Bible probably way too often. I say this because I want everyone to know that this is normal. Starting a walk with God does not happen overnight. In almost all circumstances, that walk will take you until your very last breath. Along the way, you will question your existence, God's existence, Biblical principles, and the list goes on and on. Don't worry about it if you find yourself doing some of these things. It is alright if you still have questions. The most important part is to decide to believe in Christ. God knows full well that you will have to crawl before you walk.

I was saved at a young age. Thanks to my amazing Mom and Dad, I was put in an environment where being a Christian came without persecution.

The writing of this book was part of my process of spreading the good news. I have always wanted to travel the World and be on the mission field to share about God's love. That didn't happen for me, so this book is my opportunity to do so. There is a Facebook page set up for this book, and I want to personally invite you to come over and let me know where you are at with your walk with God. I want to make myself available if you would like to pray with me or even if you're going to ask questions with me. So please come and engage; I would love to meet you.

The Facebook link to chat with me is:
www.facebook.com/YouGodDog

14 Day Reading Plan

For Encouragement and Guidance

DAY ONE

Nahum 1:7 The Lord is good,
a refuge in times of trouble.
He cares for those who trust in him

2 Corinthians 1:3-4: "Blessed be the God and Father of our Lord Jesus Christ, the Father of mercies and God of all comfort, who comforts us in all our affliction, so that we may be able to comfort those who are in any affliction, with the comfort with which we ourselves are comforted by God."

DAY TWO

Proverbs 3:5-6: "Trust in the LORD with all your heart, and do not lean on your own understanding. In all your ways acknowledge him, and he will make straight your paths."

1 Peter 2:9-10: "But you are a chosen race, a royal priesthood, a holy nation, a people for his own possession, that you may proclaim the excellencies of him who called you out of darkness into his marvelous light. Once you were not a people, but now you are God's people; once you had not received mercy, but now you have received mercy."

DAY THREE

Psalm 31:24: "Be strong, and let your heart take courage, all you who wait for the LORD!"

1 John 3:1-3: "See what kind of love the Father has given to us, that we should be called children of God; and so, we are. The reason why the world does not know us is that it did not know him. Beloved, we are God's children now, and what we will be has not yet appeared; but we know that when he appears we shall be like him, because we shall see him as he is. And everyone who thus hopes in him purifies himself as he is pure."

DAY FOUR

Proverbs 18:10: "The name of the LORD is a strong tower; the righteous man runs into it and is safe."

Philippians 3:7-9: "But whatever gain I had, I counted as loss for the sake of Christ. Indeed, I count everything as loss because of the surpassing worth of knowing Christ Jesus my Lord. For his sake I have suffered the loss of all things and count them as rubbish, in order that I may gain Christ and be found in him, not having a righteousness of my own that comes from the law, but that which comes through faith in Christ, the righteousness from God that depends on faith."

DAY FIVE

Psalm 16:8: "I have set the LORD always before me; because he is at my right hand, I shall not be shaken."

1 Peter 2:11: "Beloved, I urge you as sojourners and exiles to abstain from the passions of the flesh, which wage war against your soul."

DAY SIX

Psalm 119:114-115: "You are my hiding place and my shield; I hope in your word. Depart from me, you evildoers, that I may keep the commandments of my God."

2 Corinthians 1:3-4: "Blessed be the God and Father of our Lord Jesus Christ, the Father of mercies and God of all comfort, who comforts us in all our affliction, so that we may be able to comfort those who are in any affliction, with the comfort with which we ourselves are comforted by God."

DAY SEVEN

Psalm 23:4: "Even though I walk through the valley of the shadow of death, I will fear no evil, for you are with me; your rod and your staff, they comfort me."

Romans 12:2 Do not conform to the pattern of this world but be transformed by the renewing of your mind. Then you will be able to test and approve what God's will is—his good, pleasing and perfect will.

DAY EIGHT

Psalm 46:7: "The LORD of hosts is with us;
the God of Jacob is our fortress."

1 John 4:4 "Ye are of God, little children, and
have overcome them: because greater is he
that is in you, than he that is in the world."

DAY NINE

Psalm 55:22: "Cast your burden on the
LORD, and he will sustain you; he will never
permit the righteous to be moved."

John 16:33: "I have said these things to you,
that in me you may have peace. In the world
you will have tribulation. But take heart; I
have overcome the world."

DAY TEN

Psalm 62:6: "He only is my rock and my salvation, my fortress; I shall not be shaken."

Matthew 11:28: "Come to me, all who labor and are heavy laden, and I will give you rest."

DAY ELEVEN

Psalm 118:14-16: "The LORD is my strength and my song; he has become my salvation. Glad songs of salvation are in the tents of the righteous: 'The right hand of the LORD does valiantly, the right hand of the LORD exalts, the right hand of the LORD does valiantly!'"

Matthew 11:28: "Come to me, all who labor and are heavy laden, and I will give you rest."

DAY TWELVE

Psalm 119:50: "This is my comfort in my affliction, that your promise gives me life."

2 Timothy 1:7 For the Spirit God gave us does not make us timid, but gives us power, love and self-discipline.

DAY THIRTEEN

Psalm 56:4 In God, whose word I praise—
in God I trust and am not afraid.
What can mere mortals do to me?

Philippians 4:19: "And my God will supply
every need of yours according to his riches in
glory in Christ Jesus."

DAY FOURTEEN

Isaiah 40:31: "But they who wait for the
LORD shall renew their strength; they shall
mount up with wings like eagles; they shall
run and not be weary; they shall walk and not
faint."

Luke 12:32 "Do not be afraid, little flock, for
your Father has been pleased to give you the
kingdom

You, God, and Your Dog

God is searching for your heart. He wants to connect with you. The invitation to be safe and secure within his loving arms is always upon you and secretly peaks your interest.

If you would like to accept Christ into your heart, the first step is to say out loud that you believe. No prayer will save you, however starting with this is a great place to begin. The journey from this point on will be wonderous. Embrace the journey, my prayers go out for you as you start your new life.

Here is an age-old prayer for you to say and meditate on:

Dear Lord Jesus, I know that I am a sinner, and I ask for your forgiveness. I believe you died for my sins and rose from the dead. I turn from my sins and invite you to come into my heart and life. I want to trust and follow You as my Lord and Savior.

You, God, and Your Dog